Just for You

A Celebration of
Joy and Friendship

A Special Gift

To

Roger and Carol

From

Jeanne ♡

Date

Happy Engagement! Feb. 14, 1999

Ribbons of Love

MOTHER
Another Word for Love

GARDENS OF FRIENDSHIP

HAPPY IS THE HOUSE
That Shelters a Friend

IN THE PRESENCE OF ANGELS

JUST FOR YOU
A Celebration of Joy and Friendship

LOVING THOUGHTS
for Tender Hearts

Just for You

Brownlow

Brownlow Publishing Company, Inc.

The Greatest Friendship

By friendship I suppose you mean the greatest
love, the greatest usefulness, and the most open
communication, the noblest sufferings, and
the severest truth, the heartiest counsel,
and the greatest union of minds of
which brave men and
women are capable.

JEREMY TAYLOR

You may be deceived if you trust too much,
but you will live in torment
if you do not trust enough.

DR. FRANK CRANE

The first point of wisdom is to
discern that which is false,
the second, to know that which is true.

LANTANTIUS

A good laugh
is sunshine in a house.

WILLIAM MAKEPEACE THACKERAY

First Thoughts

Like cuttlefish we conceal ourselves, we darken
the atmosphere in which we move; we are not transparent.
I pine for one to whom I can speak my first thoughts;
thoughts which represent me truly, which are no better
and no worse than I; thoughts which have the bloom
on them, which alone can be sacred or divine.

HENRY DAVID THOREAU

What Is Life?

Your life is what you make it.
Your life can be simple if you will
set it up with simplicity as a goal!
It will take courage to cut away
from the thousand and one hindrances
that make life complex, but it can be done!

RHODA LACHAR

The only security for happiness
is to have a mind filled with the love
of the infinite and the eternal.

SPINOZA

The successful man has enthusiasm:
Good work is never done in cold blood, heat is needed
to forge anything. Every great achievement is
the story of a flaming heart.

A. B. ZU TAVERN

If you wish to astonish the whole world,
tell the simple truth.

RAHEL

*S*ome people think they are poor just because
they do not have everything they want.

ROY L. SMITH

*P*eople do not lack strength; they lack will.

VICTOR HUGO

Look well into thyself;
there is a source of strength
which will always spring up
if thou wilt always look there.

MARCUS AURELIUS

There is no death!
The stars go down to rise upon some fairer shore.

J. L. MCCREERY

True friendship is like sound health; the value
of it is seldom known until it be lost.

CHARLES CALEB COLTON

Service in a just cause rewards the worker
with more real happiness and satisfaction
than any other venture of life.

CARRIE CATT

Just One Word

All of us encounter, at least once in our life,
some individual who utters words
that make us think forever. There are men
whose phrases are oracles; who condense
in a sentence the secrets of life; who blurt
out an aphorism that forms a character,
or illustrates an existence.

BENJAMIN, EARL OF DISRAELI

If you wish to succeed,
consult three old people.

CHINESE PROVERB

*W*hen it comes to life, the critical thing is
whether you take things for granted
or take them with gratitude.

G. K. CHESTERTON

Get up every morning, look in the mirror and say,
"I'm going to make good things happen today."

JUDSON SAYRE

What we have to learn to do, we learn by doing.

ARISTOTLE

If you tell the truth
you don't have to remember anything.

MARK TWAIN

Self-control

Self-discipline is always rewarded by a strength
which brings an inexpressible, silent inner joy
which becomes the dominant tone of life.

ALEXIS CARREL

I have never met a man who has given
me as much trouble as myself.

DWIGHT L. MOODY

Self-control is the ability to keep cool
while someone is making it hot for you.

The Fruit of the Spirit Is—
Self-control

A man is his own best kingdom.
But self-control, this truest and greatest monarchy,
rarely comes by inheritance. Every one of us
must conquer himself; and we may do so,
if we take conscience for our guide and general.

JOHN LUBBOCK

Mine & Thine

Four things are the property of friendship:
love and **affection**, **security** and **joy**. And four things
must be tried in friendship: faith, intention, discretion,
and patience. Indeed, as the sage says, all men
would lead a happy life if only two tiny words
were taken from them; **mine** and **thine**.

AILRED OF RIEVAULX

$\mathcal{B}$e silent or let thy words
be worth more than silence.

PYTHAGORAS

$\mathcal{D}$on't marry for money, you can borrow it cheaper.

SCOTTISH PROVERB

$\mathcal{N}$o man is more than another unless
he does more than another.

MIGUEL DE CERVANTES

One cool judgment
is worth a thousand hasty councils.
The thing to do is to supply light and not heat.

WOODROW WILSON

A man without mirth is like a wagon
without springs... he is jolted disagreeably
by every pebble in the road.

HENRY WARD BEECHER

The way to gain a good reputation is to endeavor to be what you desire to appear.

SOCRATES

Life is so crowded with everyday. It takes great effort to step aside and just watch and think.

DAGOBERT RUNES

How often do we labor for that which satisfieth not.

JOHN LUBBOCK

Today

Every morning is a fresh beginning. Every day is the world made new. Today is a new day. Today is my world made new. I have lived all my life up to this moment, to come to this day. This moment—this day—is as good as any moment in all eternity. I shall make of this dayheaven on earth.

This is—my day

of opportunity.

DAN CUSTER

If

If there is righteousness in the heart,
there will be beauty in character,
there will be harmony in the home,
there will be order in the nation.
Where there is order in the nation,
there will be peace in the world.

CHINESE PROVERB

Meekness is not weakness.

SIR WILLIAM GURNEY BENHAM

Feelings are everywhere...
be gentle.

J. Masai

We can only be valued as we make ourselves valuable.
RALPH WALDO EMERSON

*C*olors fade, temples crumble, empires fall,
but wise words endure.
THORNDIKE

*M*ake no mistake, my friend,
it takes more than money
to make men rich.
A. P. GOUTHEY

Silence is the voice of the convinced; loudness is the voice of those who want to convince themselves.

Dagobert Runes

We all make mistakes, and if we have our eyes open we find out that they are mistakes. One of the greatest that mankind makes is to stop and worry over a mistake already made.

H. F. Kletzing

*S*uccess is not measured by the money earned
but by the service rendered.

ROY L. SMITH

*I*f you are not having problems
you are missing an opportunity for growth.

THOMAS BLANDI

Foundation of Love

Love for oneself is the foundation of a
brotherly society and personal peace of mind.
By loving oneself I do not mean coddling oneself,
indulging in vanity, conceit, self-glorification.
I do, however, insist on the necessity
of a proper self-regard as a prerequisite
of the good and moral life.

JOSHUA LIEBMAN

Put up with small annoyances to gain great results.
AMERICAN PROVERB

The high-minded man must care more for
the truth than for what people think.
ARISTOTLE

The highest reward for man's toil is not
what he gets for it but what he becomes by it.
JOHN RUSKIN

Rules for Living

Important rules to watch in living: Keep life simple.
Avoid watching for a knock in your motor.
Learn to like work. Have a good hobby. Learn to
be satisfied. Like people. Say cheerful, pleasant things.
Turn the defeat of adversity into victory.
Meet your problems with decision.
Make the present moment a success.
Always be planning something.
Say "nuts" to irritations.

JOHN SCHINDLER, M.D.

A great river is not aimless. It has
direction and purpose. So also must a good life
have a definite aim; all its strength and
fullness must be turned in one direction.

GRENVILLE KLEISER

*B*etter a meal of vegetables
where there is love than a
fattened calf with hatred.

PROVERBS 15:17

*T*rust men and they will be true to you; treat them
greatly and they will show themselves great.

RALPH WALDO EMERSON

*Y*ou are only as big as the world
you are interested in.

ROY L. SMITH

*H*e who has a firm will
molds the world to himself.

JOHANN WOLFGANG VON GOETHE

Faithfulness

Faithfulness in little things is a big thing.

JOHN CHRYSOSTOM

Faithfulness is consecration in overalls.

EVELYN UNDERHILL

**When men cease to be faithful to their God,
he who expects to find them so to each other
will be much disappointed.**

GEORGE HORNE

The Fruit of the Spirit Is—Faithfulness

Is your place a small place?
Tend it with care!—He set you there.
Is your place a large place?
Guard it with care!—He set you there.
Whate'er your place, it is
Not yours alone, but his
Who set you there.

JOHN OXENHAM

$\mathcal{N}$o one can make a real masterpiece of life
until he *sees* something infinitely greater in
his vocation than bread and butter and shelter.

O. S. MARDEN

$\mathcal{H}$e who reigns within himself and rules his
passions, desires and fears, is more than a king.

JOHN MILTON

$\mathcal{P}$lunge boldly into the thing of life.
Each lives it, not to many is it known;
and seize it where you will, it is interesting.

JOHANN WOLFGANG VON GOETHE

$\mathcal{T}$he two hardest things to handle in life
are failure and success.

UNKNOWN

Doing Right

*E*very man at the bottom of his heart
wants to do right. But only
he can do right who knows right;
only he knows right who thinks right;
only he thinks right who believes right.

TIORIO

$\mathcal{B}$ooks are the ever-burning lamps
of accumulated wisdom.

$\mathcal{P}$ractice makes perfect,
so be careful what you practice.

$\mathcal{B}$e true to your own highest conviction.

W. E. CHANNING

It Takes Time

An acorn is not an oak tree when it is sprouted.
It must go through long summers and fierce winters;
it has to endure all that frost and snow and side-striking
winds can bring before it is a full-grown oak. These are
rough teachers; but rugged schoolmasters make
rugged pupils. So a man is not a man when he
is created; he is only begun. His manhood
must come with years.

Henry Ward Beecher

Laborers Together

God has conferred upon us
a great honor–that of laboring together with Him.
It is ours to bring the word that will create new life,
build a new society, and make life more livable.

A. P. GOUTHEY

Goodness

He that does good to another man does
also good to himself; not only in the consequence,
but in the very act of doing it.
The consciousness of well-doing is an ample reward.

LUCIUS ANNAEUS SENECA

The Fruit of the Spirit Is—Goodness

Goodness consists not in the outward things we do,

but in the inward thing we are.

EDWIN HUBBEL CHAPIN

Do all the good you can, to all the people you can,

in all the ways you can, as often as ever you can,

as long as you can.

CHARLES HADDON SPURGEON

If you think "revenge is sweet," look into
the faces of those who have lived on it for years.

ROY L. SMITH

Study how to do the most good
and let the pay take care of itself.

LYMON ABBOTT

Hide not your talents, they for use were made.
What's a sundial in the shade?

BENJAMIN FRANKLIN

A faithful companion
is a sure anchor.

A man will be what his most cherished feelings are.

HENRY WARD BEECHER

God looks with favor at pure,
not full, hands.

PUBLILIUS SYRUS

In the Bible a man is measured by depth.
Man is like a tree. Everything depends on his roots.
When storms strike—the roots are the things.

RICHARD C. HALVERSON

You can make more friends in two months
by becoming interested in other people than
you can in two years by trying to get
other people interested in you.

people think, by the herd spirit, by the stereotype
into which custom and prejudice try to fit us.
We need quiet to keep in touch with ourselves,
to recharge the soul that is uniquely ours. You need
quiet to just be you, rather than a straw man.

L. R. DITZEN

Uniquely Me

Each of us, every human being in the world,
is distinct. That raw stuff of our unique selfhood
is our most precious possession. But how easily
it gets buffeted and crushed by what other

An Act of Faith

The quality of friendship, unlike that of mercy,
is continually being strained.
But it is the essence of friendship
that it can stand the strain. Friendship is like love
at its best: not blind but sympathetically
all-seeing; a support which does not wait
for understanding; an act of faith
which does not need, but always has, reason.

LOUIS UNTERMEYER

The grandest homage we can pay to truth is to use it.

RALPH WALDO EMERSON

Be yourself, and be the person you hope to be.

ROBERT LOUIS STEVENSON

When a thing is done, it's done. Don't look back.
Look forward to your next objective.

GENERAL GEORGE C. MARSHALL

Kindness

Kindness is the golden chain
by which society is bound together.

JOHANN WOLFGANG VON GOETHE

Kindness is a language which the
deaf can hear and the blind can read.

MARK TWAIN

The Fruit of the Spirit Is—Kindness

You may be sorry that you spoke,
Sorry you stayed or went,
Sorry you won or lost,
Perhaps, sorry so much was spent.
But as you go through life, you'll find
You're never sorry you were kind.

ANONYMOUS

*P*leasures are enhanced that are sparingly enjoyed.

JUVENAL

*S*teady nerves and a quiet mind are not things
we go out and find; they are things we create.

JOHN MILLER

Life begins each morning...
Each morning is the open door to a new world—
new vistas, new aims, new tryings.

LEIGH HODGES

Great works are performed not by strength
but by perseverance.

JOHNSON

To be able to look back upon one's past life
with satisfaction is to live twice.

MARTIAL

Genius begins great works;
labor alone finishes them.

JOSEPH JOUBERT

It is not permitted us
to know all things.

HORACE

*E*verything that is done in the world is done by hope.

MARTIN LUTHER

*T*o give real service you must add something
which cannot be bought or measured with money,
and that is sincerity and integrity.

DONALD A. ADAMS

The Power of a Thought

Our best friends and our worst enemies
are our thoughts. A thought can do us
more good than a doctor or a banker
or a faithful friend. It can also do us
more harm than a brick.

DR. FRANK CRANE

Simplicity is making the journey of this life
with just baggage enough.

CHARLES WARNER

Delight yourself in the Lord
and he will give you the
desires of your heart.

PSALM 37:4

$\mathcal{F}$ame is a vapor, popularity an accident,
riches take wings, those who cheer today will
curse tomorrow, only one thing endures—character.

HORACE GREELEY

$\mathcal{A}$ family will hold together across the years if each
member refrains from pointing the accusing finger.

JOHN MILLER

Patience

"Take your needle, my child, and work at
your pattern; it will come out a rose by and by."
Life is like that; one stitch at a time
taken patiently, and the pattern will
come out all right like embroidery.

OLIVER WENDELL HOLMES

The Fruit of the Spirit Is—Patience

Patience is the companion of wisdom.

ST. AUGUSTINE

Never think that God's delays are God's denials.
Hold on; hold fast; hold out. Patience is genius.

COMTE GEORGES-LOUIS LECLERC DE BUFFON

God often permits us to be perplexed
so that we may learn patience.

T. J. BACH

In Our Quietness

Character is not built by battling
and excitement alone. The harvest is not ripened by
the thunderous forces of nature, but by the secret silent
invisible forces. So the best qualities of our spiritual lives
are matured by quietness, silence and commonplace.

A. P. GOUTHEY

*W*hile you seek new friendships,
take care to cultivate the old.

*T*ears are the safety valve of the heart
when too much pressure is laid on.

ALBERT SMITH

*O*ur ideals are the blueprints of our lives.

ROY L. SMITH

What Is Love?

Love is eternal—the aspect may change, but not the essence. There is the same difference in a person before and after he is in love as there is in an unlighted lamp and one that is burning. The lamp was there and was a good lamp, but now it is shedding light too, and that is its real function. And love makes one calmer about many things, and that way, one is more fit for one's work.

VINCENT VAN GOGH

Life Is Large

Life is large. We cannot possibly grasp the
whole of it in the few years that we have to live.
What is vital? What is essential?
What may be profitably let go?
Let us ask ourselves these questions today.

ANNA LINDSAY

*I*f you wish to know the mind of a man,
listen to his words.

<small>CHINESE PROVERB</small>

*L*ife will give you what you ask of her if only
you ask long enough and plainly enough.

<small>E. NESBIT</small>

A single thought in the morning
may fill our whole day with joy and
sunshine, or gloom and depression.

PARMANDANDA

Peace

There will be peace in the world so far
as there is righteousness in the heart.

JOHN MILLER

The Fruit of the Spirit Is—Peace

This is the gift that God reserves for His special
protégés. Talent and beauty He gives to many.
Wealth is commonplace, fame not rare.
But peace of mind — that is His final
guerdon of approval, the fondest sign of His love.
Most men are never blessed with it, others wait
all their lives — yes, far into advanced age —
for this gift to descend upon them.

JOSHUA LIEBMAN

We win by tenderness;
we conquer by forgiveness.

F. W. ROBERTSON

All the Constitution guarantees
is the pursuit of happiness. You have to
catch up with it yourself.

ANONYMOUS

The hopeful man sees success
where others see failure, sunshine
where others see shadows and storm.

O. S. MARDEN

Light is the task
when many share
the toil.

HOMER

The most useful
is the greatest.

THEODORE PARKER

My Prayer

Help us, God, and give us light so that
we don't stand in our own way;
let us do from morning till night what
should be done, and give us clear ideas
of the consequences of our actions.

JOHANN WOLFGANG VON GOETHE

The duty to our neighbor
is part of our duty to God.

JOHN LUBBOCK

The most useless thing
you can give is an excuse.

ROY L. SMITH

$\mathcal{H}$eaven is not reached at a single bound;
but we build the ladder by which we rise
from the lowly earth to the vaulted skies
and we mount to its summit
round by round.

J. G. HOLLAND

*Thinking is easy, acting is difficult,
and to put one's thoughts into action
is the most difficult thing in the world.*

JOHANN WOLFGANG VON GOETHE

and doesn't know anything about.
The Lord gives his people perpetual joy
when they walk in obedience to him.

DWIGHT L. MOODY

Joy

Happiness is caused by things that happen
around me, and circumstances will mar it;
but joy flows right on through trouble;
joy flows on through the dark; joy flows
in the night as well as in the day;
joy flows all through persecution and opposition.
It is an unceasing fountain bubbling up
in the heart; a secret spring the world can't see

Out of the will of God there is
no such thing as success; in the will
of God there cannot be any failure.

ANONYMOUS

Life is not complex.
We are complex.
Life is simple and the
simple thing is the right thing.

OSCAR WILDE

To win an argument
is to lose a friend.

Nothing is more simple than greatness;
indeed, to be simple is to be great.

RALPH WALDO EMERSON

The family is the nucleus of civilization.

WILL DURANT

The word *joy* is too great and grand to be confused
with the superficial things we call happiness.

KIRBY PAGE

The Happy People

Who are the happiest people on earth?
A craftsman or artist whistling over a job well done.
A little child building sand castles. A mother,
after a busy day, bathing her baby.
A doctor who has finished a difficult and
dangerous operation, and saved a human life.
Happiness lies in a constructive job well done.

A wise man thinks before he speaks
what he ought to say; the fool speaks
and thinks afterwards what he has said.

<small>FRENCH PROVERB</small>

*T*he vision that you glorify in your mind,
the ideal that you enthrone in your heart—this you
will build your life by, this you will become.

<small>JAMES ALLEN</small>

Our necessities are few but our wants are endless.

H. W. SHAW

Music washes away from the soul
the dust of everyday life.

AUERBACH

Honest praise is most appreciated from those
who are the most worthy of it themselves.

ROY L. SMITH

Love

The great tragedy of life is not that men perish,

but that they cease to love.

SOMERSET MAUGHAM

Forgetting oneself is not a refinement of love.

It is a first condition of love.

LEON JOSEPH SUENENS

The Fruit of the Spirit Is—Love

Love is the one ingredient of which our world
never tires and of which there is never an abundance.
It is needed in the marketplace and in the mansions.
It is needed in the ghettos and in the governments.
It is needed in homes, in hospitals, and in individual hearts.
The world will never outgrow its need for love.

C. NEIL STRAIT

Give Me Light

I said to the man who stood at the gate
of the year: "Give me a light that I may tread safely
into the unknown." And he replied: "Go out into the
darkness, and put thine hand into the hand of God.
That shall be to thee better than light and
safer than a known way."

LOUISE HASKINS

In taking revenge a man is but even
with his enemy, but in passing it over
he is superior, for it is a prince's part to pardon.

SIR FRANCIS BACON

Too many people are thinking of
security instead of opportunity. They seem
more afraid of life than death.

JAMES F. BYRNES

Life is the childhood of our immortality.

JOHANN WOLFGANG VON GOETHE

Knowledge is better than riches.

AFRICAN PROVERB

To be content with what we possess
is the greatest and most secure of riches.

MARCUS TULLIUS CICERO